GUITAR *signature licks*®

essential
jazz guitar

by JOE CHARUPAKORN

ISBN 978-0-634-09095-0

HAL•LEONARD®
CORPORATION

7777 W. BLUEMOUND RD. P.O. BOX 13819 MILWAUKEE, WI 53213

Visit Hal Leonard Online at
www.halleonard.com

CONTENTS

INTRODUCTION

Jazz is an improvisational style of music based in large part on aural tradition. While some pedagogues have codified the teaching of the jazz language into a system based on classical theory, many jazz greats mastered their craft simply through learning favorite solos off recordings. The indisputable masters of jazz guitar—Wes Montgomery, Johnny Smith, Barney Kessel, Jim Hall, and Tal Farlow—all learned how to play by initially copying Charlie Christian's solos.

As a musical language, jazz is constantly expanding with each player continually adding his/her own unique stamp.

Regardless of evolution, however, jazz is a very distinct language with specific characteristics and clichés that differentiate it from other forms of improvised music. The music in this volume of *Signature Licks: Essential Jazz Guitar* was carefully chosen from classic and fundamental jazz guitar recordings to provide a solid foundation into the vernacular of swing, bebop, and post-bop guitar styles. Diligent study of the selections via dissection of key phrases, rhythms, and licks will expand your vocabulary and provide insight into the approaches and thought process used in creating these masterful performances. The included analyses accompanying each selection also highlight notable phrases and gestures. Above each figure, time boxes refer to the place in the original recording where that section appears.

DISCOGRAPHY

The songs on the accompanying audio CD include the following:

"Flying Home" – Charlie Christian, *Benny Goodman Sextet* 1939/1941
"Impressions" – Pat Martino, *Consciousness*
"In a Mellow Tone" – Joe Pass, *Portraits of Duke Ellington*
"Lover Man (Oh, Where Can You Be?)" – Django Reinhardt, *Djangology*
"Moonlight in Vermont" – Johnny Smith, *Moonlight in Vermont*
"On a Slow Boat to China" – Barney Kessel, *Kessel Plays Standards*
"Speak Low" – Grant Green, *I Want to Hold Your Hand*
"Stompin' at the Savoy" – Jim Hall, *Jazz Guitar*
"There Is No Greater Love" – Tal Farlow, *Tal*
"The Way You Look Tonight" – Wes Montgomery, *The Alternative Wes Montgomery*

THE RECORDING

Doug Boduch:	guitar
Louis Cucunato:	piano
Tom McGirr:	bass
Ben Hans:	drums
Jerry Loughney:	violin

Recorded at Beathouse Music, Milwaukee, WI
Produced by Jim Reith

ABOUT THE AUTHOR

Joe Charupakorn is a guitarist, composer, author, and editor. He has authored and edited numerous books, including *Signature Licks: The Best of Django Reinhardt*, published by Hal Leonard Corporation. He is an endorser of Peavey, Radial Engineering Ltd., Pedaltrain, and LaBella Strings, and currently resides in New York City. Visit him on the web at www.joecharupakorn.com

ARTIST BIOGRAPHIES

Charlie Christian

In a span of three short years (1939–1942) Charlie Christian single-handedly revolutionized the course of jazz guitar. Prior to Christian, jazz guitarists were primarily relegated to an accompanying role, comping four-to-the-bar in a big-band rhythm section. Christian broke the mold by playing melodic, single-note solos that stood toe-to-toe with the horn players. His groundbreaking playing brought the guitar into the limelight and opened the floodgates for the next generation of jazz guitarists like Wes Montgomery, Jim Hall, and Joe Pass, who all cited Christian as a major influence. (In fact, Montgomery picked up the guitar after hearing Christian's "Solo Flight.")

Charlie Christian was born on July 29, 1916 in Bonham, Texas into a family of musicians. His father supported the family by playing sacred music on stringed instruments. Christian's introduction to the guitar came in the form of an eleven-string Symphony Harp, which he would strum while dozing off on his father's lap. On November 11, 1918, the Christian family moved to Oklahoma City, Oklahoma.

It was there that Christian started his musical career, playing for tips (with a quartet comprised of Charlie, his two brothers, and father) in local cafés. His career flourished, and in 1939, at the urging of arranger Mary Lou Williams, Columbia Records associate recording director John Hammond flew out to hear Charlie. Hammond was so impressed he set Christian up with an audition for Benny Goodman, the "King of Swing." Initially, Goodman, who had no intention of auditioning him, dismissed Christian. But two days later during Goodman's gig at the Victor Hugo restaurant in Beverly Hills, Christian sneaked his way on stage (with the help of Hammond and bassist Artie Bernstein) and tore the house down with his incendiary solo on "Rose Room." Christian got the gig, and the landscape of jazz guitar would be forever altered.

Pat Martino

Pat Martino's influence upon the jazz guitar world is indelible. His legendary *moto perpetuo* licks and super-formidable picking technique have both inspired and terrified hordes of jazz guitarists, sending many back to the woodshed. In *Guitar Player* magazine, contemporary jazz guitar sensation Russell Malone said—referring to some classic albums, which included Martino's *Consciousness*—"I would sit by the record player and try to copy their licks. I'd just play them over and over again until I got it where I wanted it to be. It took maybe three or four years of constantly doing that before I got my chops together." That same course of study has been taken by scores of jazz guitarists, with Martino being among the most highly emulated of guitarists.

Born Pat Azzara, in Philadelphia, PA, in 1944, Martino was introduced to the guitar at age twelve by his father, who had studied with Eddie Lang. Martino's first guitar was a pawn shop special that his father gave him with the promise of a real guitar if Martino displayed promise. Six weeks later his father was sufficiently impressed and bought him a Gibson Les Paul Standard. Martino took lessons with Dennis Sandole (with whom John Coltrane also studied during the same time period), practiced assiduously, and by the time he was fifteen had turned pro. Martino scored a gig with organist Charles Earland and eventually moved to New York City, landing gigs as a sideman for organists Jimmy Smith, "Brother" Jack McDuff, and Don Patterson. In 1967, Martino released *El Hombre*, the first in a series of albums for Prestige Records.

Around 1980, Martino suffered an aneurysm that rendered him amnesic. He completely forgot how to play the guitar. Miraculously, he eventually re-learned, and by 1987 released an album entitled *The Return*. Ten years later, he recorded *All Sides Now*, a Blue Note release featuring artists as disparate as shredder Joe Satriani, the late Michael Hedges, Les Paul, and vocalist Cassandra Wilson. In 2004, he won the *Downbeat* magazine reader's poll for Guitar Player of the Year. To this day Martino continues to inspire and awe.

Joe Pass

Joe Pass's mastery of jazz guitar was all-encompassing, embracing every possible situation—solo, with an ensemble, and as a vocal accompanist—with unflinching virtuosity and authority. Joe was among the elite in jazz circles, performing and recording with a veritable who's-who of jazz giants: Oscar Peterson, Ella Fitzgerald, Sarah Vaughan, Duke Ellington, Count Basie, Dizzy Gillespie, and Benny Goodman, to name a few.

Born on January 13, 1929, in New Brunswick, New Jersey, Joe grew up in a dreary blue-collar Pennsylvania town where his father worked in a steel mill. Hoping for a better life for Pass, his father forced him to endure grueling practice sessions during his teen years, with eight-hour days being the norm. This paid off many times over, as Pass developed an amazing command of both the instrument and the jazz language.

Early in his career, Joe developed a heroin addiction that eventually landed him in rehab at Synanon. After his recovery he named his first album as a leader *Sounds of Synanon*. He would go on to become a household name in jazz with albums like *For Django* and the landmark *Virtuoso*, the first in a series of brilliant solo guitar albums. Pass lost a two-year battle with liver cancer and passed away on May 23, 1994.

Django Reinhardt

Django Reinhardt's hyper-virtuosic playing, phoenix-like comeback, and unconventional persona have left the jazz world with an icon of near-mythic proportions. His musical beginnings started at age twelve when he received a banjo from Raclot, a neighbor. Reinhardt taught himself how to play and gradually became a part of the Parisian music scene, rubbing elbows with all of the local pros. He made his first recording at age eighteen with accordionist Jean Vaissade. His star continued to rise until November 2, 1928, when a life-altering event took place. Reinhardt accidentally dropped a candle in his caravan, and a massive fire erupted, leaving him severely injured. His left hand was badly mangled, and the odds of regaining finger movement seemed highly improbable. Reinhardt's guitar playing days appeared to be over.

In the hospital Reinhardt would try to play the guitar, only to be met with unbearable frustration. However, with the survival instinct running in his gypsy blood, Reinhardt persisted until he eventually regained the use of his thumb, index, and middle fingers. By 1933 he was playing with violinist Stephane Grapelli in the Quintet of the Hot Club of France and receiving international acclaim. As he continued to achieve greater success, his guitar playing evolved to encompass elements of bebop. On May 15, 1953 Reinhardt died of a stroke at the tender age of forty-three. Many consider him to be the most influential European in jazz history.

Johnny Smith

Johnny Smith's guitar playing epitomizes elegance and grace. His album, *Moonlight in Vermont*, was voted Album of the Year by *Downbeat* magazine and is among the most essential of jazz guitar recordings. Born on June 25, 1922, in Birmingham, Alabama, Smith grew up hearing the sounds of his father's banjo. Under the influence of Django Reinhardt and Charlie Christian, Smith taught himself how to play guitar. By age twenty-five, he landed a gig performing, composing, and arranging with the NBC Orchestra in New York City.

Smith's stint at NBC lasted until 1958. His wife died, and to be closer to his daughter, he packed his bags and left the Big Apple for Colorado. This move paralleled Tal Farlow's departure from the spotlight at roughly the same time. Smith, with his immense disdain for big city life, remains in Colorado.

Barney Kessel

Barney Kessel was a master guitarist and an important figure in the jazz guitar lineage. He was born October 17, 1923, in Muskogee, Oklahoma—the state where Charlie Christian, the founding father of jazz guitar, came to prominence. Kessel idolized Christian and studied his playing style intently, eventually taking Christian's place in a local band. Shortly thereafter, Kessel played with Christian at a jam session and had an epiphany—he had to find his own voice on the guitar. Kessel gradually developed a distinct sound and, at Christian's encouragement, moved to Los Angeles, California, where he joined the Chico Marx Orchestra.

The musical climate in L.A. allowed Kessel greater exposure and playing opportunities. He performed and recorded with the greats of swing and bebop—the Artie Shaw Orchestra, the Benny Goodman Orchestra, Billie Holiday, and Charlie Parker—and he was the first guitarist with the Oscar Peterson Trio. Kessel was also a first-call studio musician who can be heard on recordings by Frank Sinatra, Elvis Presley, and Liberace, among others. His illustrious career spanned several decades and encompassed styles like swing, bebop, and cool jazz. In 1992, a stroke ended his playing career and on May 6, 2004, he died of brain cancer. Kessel's recordings continue to impact the jazz guitar world.

Grant Green

Grant Green is a guitarist's guitarist. Not nearly the household name that others like Wes Montgomery or George Benson have become, Grant Green is the underdog of jazz guitar, achieving cult-like status among scores of jazz musicians.

Born June 6, 1935, in St. Louis, Missouri, Grant Green was exposed to the guitar via his musical family (his father and uncle were both guitarists). Initial stints playing gospel, boogie-woogie, and rock 'n' roll eventually developed into an interest in jazz; Green viewed all of these styles as an extension of the blues. His first record date (with tenor saxophonist Jimmy Forrest) soon followed. Later, tenor saxophonist Lou Donaldson heard him playing in East St. Louis and was so impressed he introduced Green to Blue Note founder Alfred Lion. This marked the beginning of Green's illustrious recording career (both as a leader and as a sideman), which totaled ninety-three records.

Like many of his peers, Green suffered a career-long battle with drug addiction. His severe addiction interrupted his career from 1967–1969, a portion of which was spent in jail. The addiction eventually took a debilitating toll on Green's health, and for most of 1978 he was bed ridden in a hospital. Against doctor's orders Green resumed touring in 1979. On January 31, 1979, at the age of forty-three, Green died of cardiac arrest. In an interesting and perhaps ironic coincidence, Wes Montgomery died at the same age.

Jim Hall

Jim Hall is considered by many to be the greatest living jazz guitarist. His creative and organic approach is a welcome contrast to the myopic purism that can plague young beboppers and staunch traditionalists. Hall embraces the music of John Coltrane and Charlie Parker with equal reverence for Wolfgang Amadeus Mozart and Paul Hindemith. His broad musical scope has made him the guitarist of choice among jazz immortals like Bill Evans (with whom he recorded the critically acclaimed albums *Undercurrent* and *Intermodulation*) and Sonny Rollins (Hall's groundbreaking playing on Rollins's 1962 return album *The Bridge* is especially influential to jazz guitarists).

Born December 4, 1930, in Buffalo, New York, he grew up to the sounds of his Uncle Ed—for whom Hall named a tune, on his Telarc release *Dialogues* (recorded with guitar phenom Mike Stern)—singing "Wabash Cannonball" around the house. Hall picked up the guitar and after hearing Charlie Christian's "Solo Flight" at age thirteen was, to paraphrase Hall, addicted. Coincidentally, it was the same recording that set off Wes Montgomery.

He would later enroll at the Cleveland Institute of Music where, as a music theory student, he studied eclectic musical styles like serialism and medieval music. Hall headed to Los Angeles, California after graduating and joined the Chico Hamilton Quintet in 1955. Five years later, he relocated to New York City, the jazz capital of the world, and proceeded to make his mark. Almost fifty years later, Hall still continues to perform and compose at a very high level. He is among the jazz elite.

Tal Farlow

Tal Farlow was a hard-bop guitarist *par excellence*. Referred to as "the most complete musician I know on the guitar" by none other than Jim Hall, Farlow's playing has influenced scores of guitarists. Interestingly, Farlow never really sought to be a musician. His introduction to the guitar came via his dad's mandolin (which was tuned like a ukulele), but he didn't seriously take up the guitar until after hearing Charlie Christian at age twenty-two. He was so taken by Christian's playing that he arranged his work hours so he wouldn't miss Christian's live broadcasts. He studied Christian's solos, learning them note-for-note.

After Christian passed, Farlow found inspiration in tenor saxophonist Lester Young and piano virtuoso Art Tatum. Farlow's big break came in 1949 when he joined the Red Norvo trio, which also featured Charles Mingus. Farlow quickly got his chops together to keep up with Norvo's speedy style and became one of the leading jazz guitarists of the 1950s.

In 1958, at the height of his newfound glory, Farlow turned his back on the spotlight. He left the hectic scene completely, moving to Sea Bright, New Jersey, to resume his original vocation of painting signs. He still played locally, occasionally recording and performing at festivals. On July 25, 1998, he fell victim to esophageal cancer and passed away.

The two years that preceded Farlow's death were highly eventful for him. He remarried in 1997, and a year earlier a seventy-fifth birthday concert in Farlow's honor took place as part of the JVC Jazz Festival at Merkin Concert Hall in New York City. This concert featured jazz greats like Attila Zoller, Herb Ellis, and Johnny Smith. As witness to the event, I can personally attest that the tribute was outstanding, once again confirming Farlow's influence on the jazz community.

Wes Montgomery

Wes Montgomery has perhaps had the most direct effect on the sound of contemporary jazz guitar. His impact is incalculable, influencing virtually every jazz guitarist that followed him. Legends Jim Hall and George Benson, and prominent masters like Pat Metheny and Mike Stern sing his praises, and the study of his playing is integral to the education of every jazz guitarist.

Born John Leslie Montgomery on March 6, 1925, in Indianapolis, he picked up the guitar at the late age of nineteen after hearing Charlie Christian's "Solo Flight." Montgomery immersed himself in Christian's solos and learned them note-for-note by ear. Within a year he played Christian's solos at the 440 club in Indianapolis.

He later scored a gig with Lionel Hampton that paved the way for his future success. Montgomery was a family man however, and chose his family over the road, eventually giving up the gig. Back in Indianapolis, Montgomery worked a grueling job at a radio-parts factory from 7 AM to 3 PM and would gig at the Turf Bar from 9 PM to 5AM, leaving him virtually no time to rest.

On September 7, 1949, Montgomery met alto saxophonist Cannonball Adderley—an event that proved to be propitious. At the urging of Adderley, Riverside Records gave Montgomery a record deal, and a legend was born. Montgomery's recorded output with Riverside—particularly *The Incredible Jazz Guitar of Wes Montgomery*—astounded musicians and critics. In 1965, Montgomery signed with Verve and recorded more commercial music that targeted a mainstream audience. His core audience was put off somewhat by the syrupy arrangements of these records, but Montgomery became a celebrity and gained greater financial security. He passed away on June 15, 1968, but remains a true giant of jazz guitar.

FLYING HOME

Music by Benny Goodman and Lionel Hampton

Sextet: Charlie Christian, guitar; Benny Goodman, clarinet; Lionel Hampton, vibes;
Artie Bernstein, bass; Fletcher Henderson, piano; Nick Fatool, drums.

Figure 1—Head

   "Flying Home," the jubilant swing classic penned by Benny Goodman and Lionel
Hampton, serves as a vehicle for classic improvisational excursions by Goodman,
Hampton, and Christian. Written in standard AABA form, the tune never strays too far from
the tonic key of E♭. Harmonically, the A section consists of a descending bass line written
around a I–IV–V progression with inversions. The B section uses the same progression
but with an augmented harmonic rhythm and a few twists. Christian (doubled by vibes)
phrases the A section melodies with slides to create a sax-like legato sound. For the B
section, Christian comps in straight quarter notes, and Goodman takes over the melody
(arranged here for guitar).

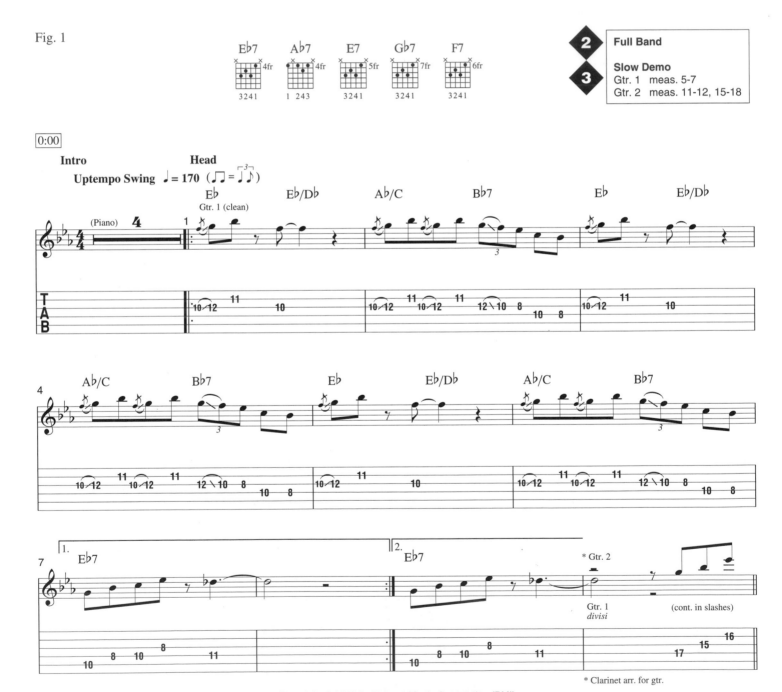

Figure 2—Guitar Solo and Vibraphone Solo

Christian's soloing style paved the way for future generations of guitarists to come. His bluesy phrasing and sense of swing were highly emulated, and his lines became part of the jazz lexicon. His "Flying Home" solo starts with a line derived from the Eb major pentatonic scale (Eb–F–G–Bb–C). Christian makes judicious use of the bluesy minor 3rd (Gb) as a leading tone into the major 3rd (G) in measures 1–2. This half-step approach recurs throughout the solo.

The antecedent-consequent phrasing of the opening measures (measures 1–2 and 3–4) give the solo cohesiveness. In measure 13, Christian starts his phrase with a simple quarter-note rhythm. Observe how the rhythm gets shifted to the upbeats in measures 15–16, and how this rhythmic shift sets up Christian's eighth-note runs for the B section (measures 17–24). The use of chromaticism in measures 20–22 also add to the intensity. Measures 25–26 and 27–28 contain antecedent-consequent phrasing similar to that heard at the start of the solo. A bend to the b3rd (Gb) is played in measure 29, bringing the solo to a close with a familiar bluesy sound.

For Lionel Hampton's vibraphone solo (arranged here for guitar), Christian plays a figure comprised of three notes (Gb, C, and Eb), accenting the upbeats. Christian employs this harmonically static figure against the underlying chord progression to great effect. The sharp, staccato attacks act as rhythmic counterpoint to the rest of the rhythm section. In measures 39–40, Hampton rhythmically catches the upbeat accents in his phrase. In measures 47–49 Hampton again accentuates the upbeats.

Fig. 2

Full Band

Slow Demo
Gtr. 1 meas. 1-8, 11-12, 17-24

[0:52]

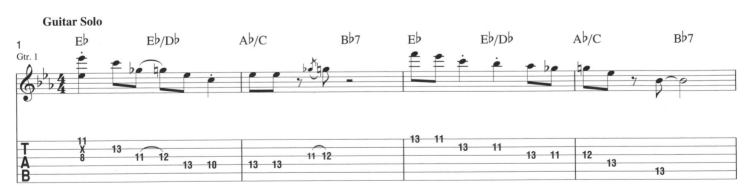

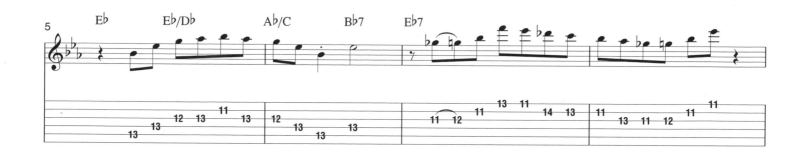

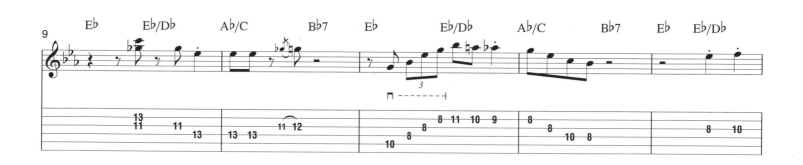

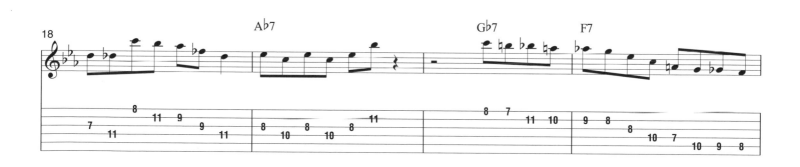

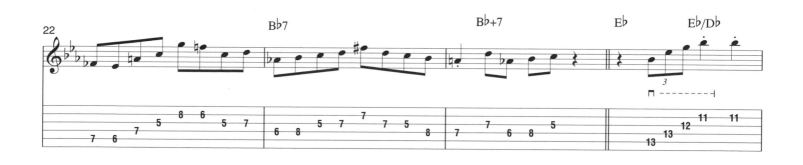

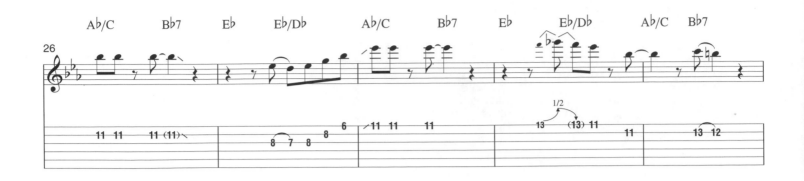

Vibraphone Solo

* Vibes arr. for gtr.

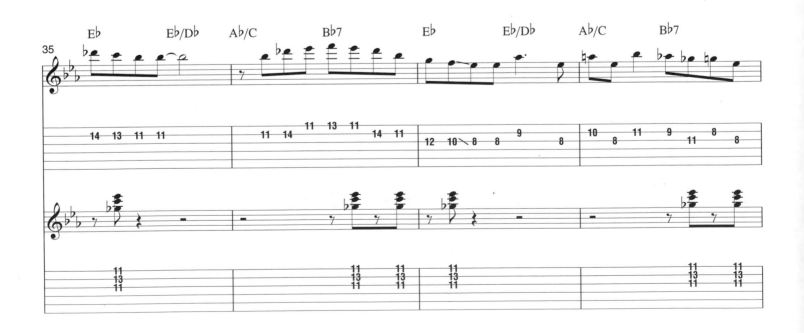

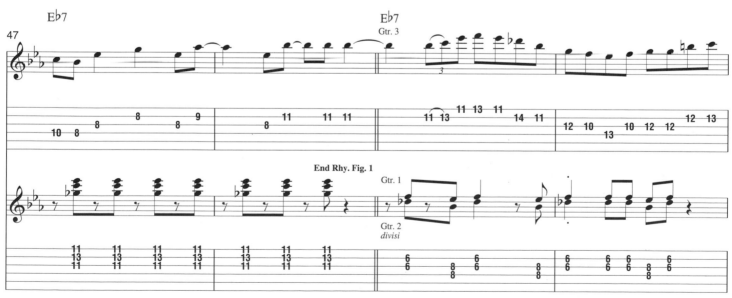

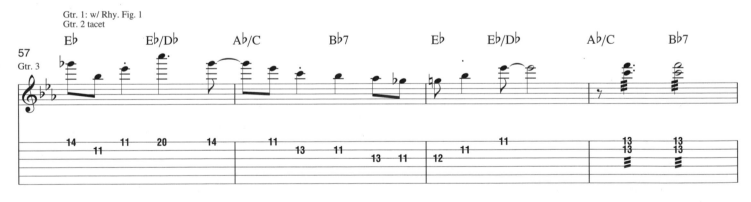

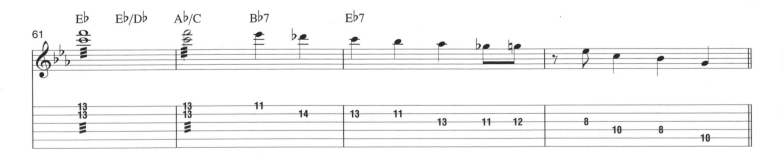

IMPRESSIONS

By John Coltrane

Quartet: Pat Martino, guitar; Eddie Green, electric piano;
Tyrone Brown, bass; Sherman Ferguson, drums.

Figure 3—Intro and Head

Pat Martino's take on "Impressions," John Coltrane's up-tempo modal classic, is an ideal showcase for his limitless technique and innate gift for melodic invention. For the eight-measure intro, Martino employs two triads to imply the A Dorian mode (A–B–C–D–E–F♯–G). Over the A pedal, the first triad (C) yields the ♭3rd (C), 5th (E), and ♭7th (G), of the tonic chord, while the second triad (Bm) results in the 9th (B), 11th (D), and 13th (F♯)—color tones that characterize the Dorian mode when used in conjunction with a m7 chord. In measures 4 and 8, the dominant chord E7♯9 confirms the A tonal center.

For the head, the bass shifts gears from the open feel of the intro to an up-tempo walking bass line. Martino plays the head fairly straightforward with a variation of the Dorian triads from the intro—the C triad is now changed to C minor—used to punctuate the phrases in measures 16–17 and 37 into the solo. The C minor triad serves a dual purpose; it functions as a half-step approach to the B minor triad and also contains the flatted 5th (E♭) to create a bluesy sound.

Fig. 3

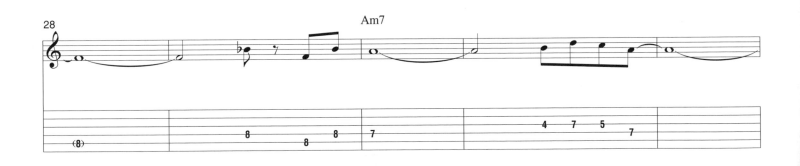

Figure 4—Guitar Solo

Based on only two chords, Am7 and B♭m7 (transposed from the original Dm7 and E♭m7 chords in Coltrane's compositions), "Impressions" presents the improviser with the challenge of maintaining interest without the harmonic guide of a chord progression. Skilled improvisers often employ elements such as chromaticism, "outside" playing, and rhythmic devices as a means of effectively tackling this tune.

In Martino's blistering solo, many of these devices are exploited to great effect. Martino uses chromatic passing tones in measures 11–14, 19–20, 28–29, 31–32, 37, 50–51, 55–60, 65–69, 90–93 ("Flight of the Bumblebee" quote), 99–101, 109, and 126–127 to add momentum to his lines. In measures 70–74 he superimposes a Cmaj7♯5 arpeggio over the Am7 chord to create an Am(maj9) sound (C–E–G♯–B = ♭3–5–7–9). Martino goes "outside" the tonality by playing (over Am7) an intervallic line based on the C minor pentatonic scale (C–E♭–F–G–B♭) in measures 34–35 and a phrase based on a hybrid of the C melodic minor scale (C–D–E♭–F–G–A–B) and the C Dorian mode (C–D–E♭–F–G–A–B♭) in measures 105–110.

Rhythmically, Martino shakes things up by creating a *hemiola* (a cross-rhythm that results from a simple meter being superimposed over a compound meter or vice versa) in measures 37–48 and 81–84. Martino often uses repeating lines like the one in measures 37–48 (and variations of it) as a means of building tension. Its repetitive nature also adds a welcome contrast to Martino's intricate, sinuous lines.

Fig. 4

8 **Full Band**

9 **Slow Demo**
Gtr. 1   9-23, 25-32,
33-60, 62-63, 65-76,
81-95, 96-128

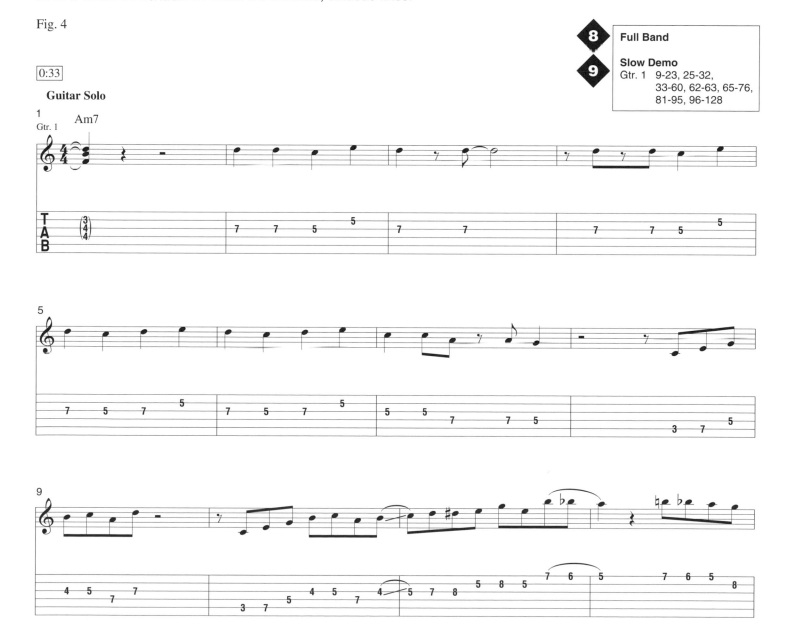

19

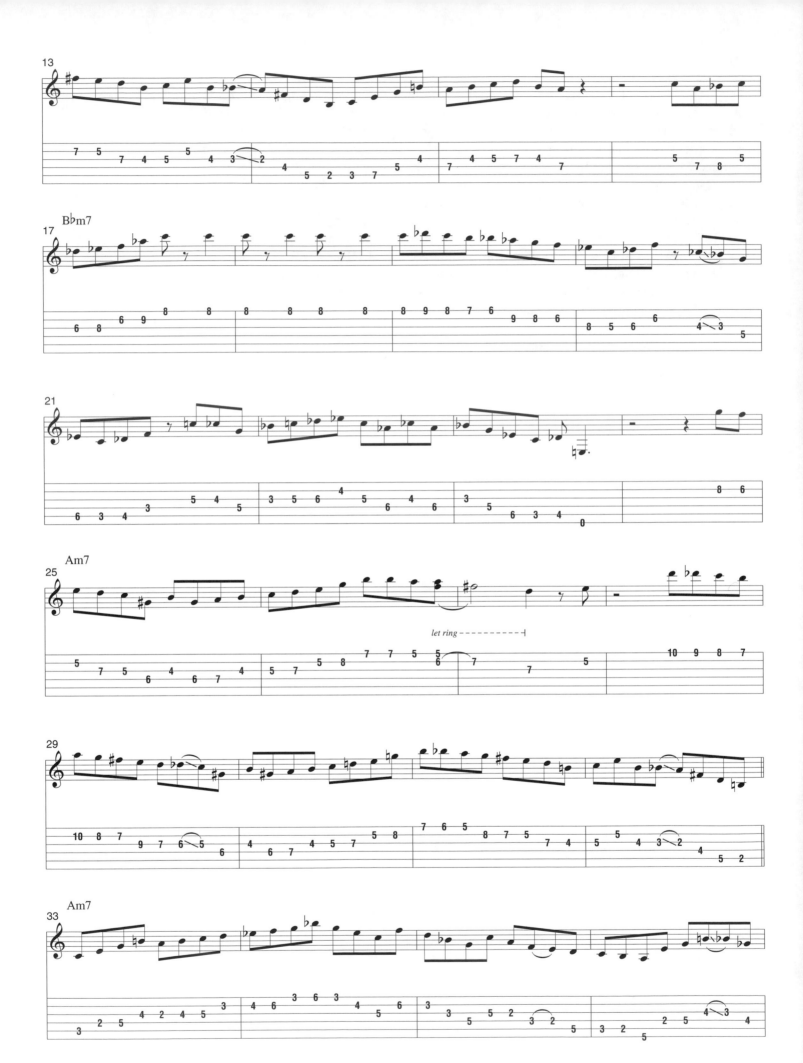

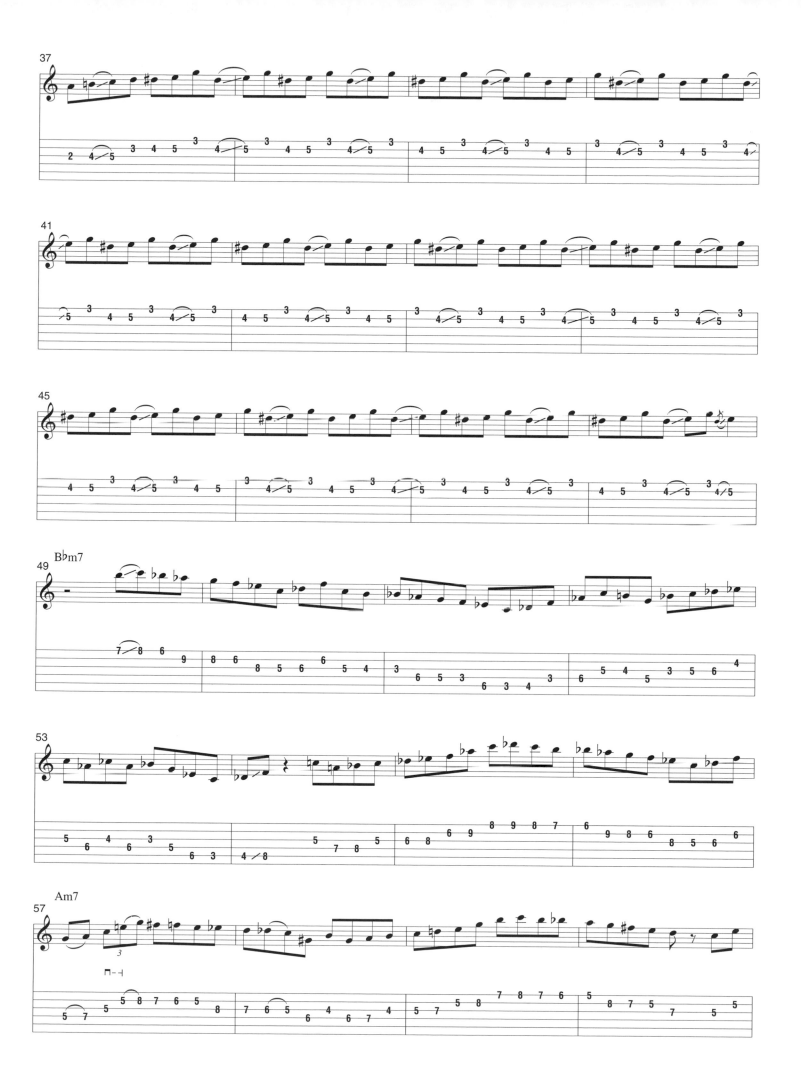

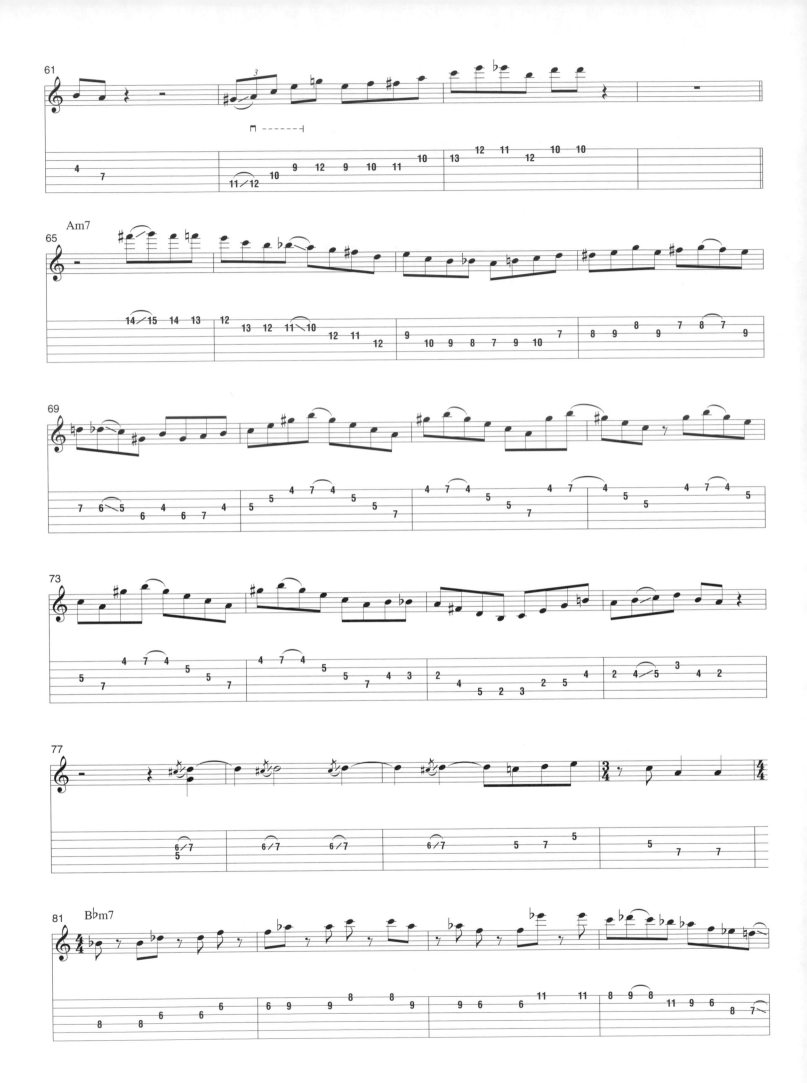

IN A MELLOW TONE

By Duke Ellington

Trio: Joe Pass, guitar; Ray Brown, bass; Bobby Durham, drums.

Figure 5—Head and Guitar Solo

In addition to his sheer command of the guitar and remarkable technical facility, Joe Pass is revered for his high level of musicianship. His performances are exquisite. At times his improvisations are so perfectly developed they sound like mini-compositions. Pass's performance on "In a Mellow Tone" from the classic *Portraits of Duke Ellington* album has that elusive quality.

The head takes on a conversational quality with Pass and bassist Ray Brown interacting in a call-and-response fashion. This approach requires listening and communication on the part of each musician, as every move is integral to the outcome and overplaying is a serious concern. Rather than play a conventional bass line during the head, Brown reacts to Pass's lines by initially playing bluesy melodies when Pass is tacet and vice versa. Brown's playing gradually becomes more concentrated and sets the stage for the solo section, where he plays a propulsive walking bass line.

Pass's solo has it all—intricate lines, bluesy gestures, chordal phrases—and it really swings! He starts off with a strong pickup statement using a simple repetition of the A♭ tonic in quarter notes (measures 31–32). This is recalled in measures 40–43 and measures 95–96 in a more active, rhythmic version. Note the bluesy use of leading tones in measures 34–35, 47–48, 82, and 84–85. Leading tones are also used in conjunction with falling tones in measures 51–53 to outline A♭6 in a wide-interval lick.

Throughout the solo Pass makes frequent use of the F blues scale (F–A♭–B♭–B–C–E♭) as a resource. The simplicity of his blues scale ideas offsets the density of his longer, harmonically-informed phrases, resulting in a balanced performance. In measures 56–69, Pass's playing is reminiscent of Wes Montgomery's call–and–response passages. Here, catchy blues riffs are followed by chord punctuations to simulate a big-band horn section. This approach is particularly effective when there is no other harmonic instrument in the ensemble.

Fig. 5

10 Full Band

11 Slow Demo
Gtr. 1 meas. 13-16, 21-24, 35-40, 45-48, 73-81

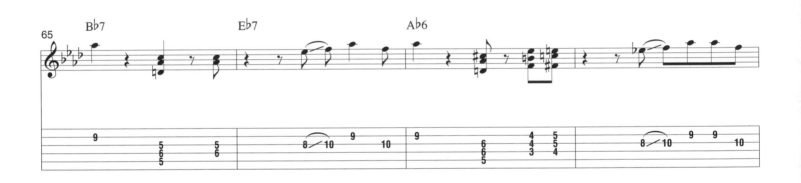

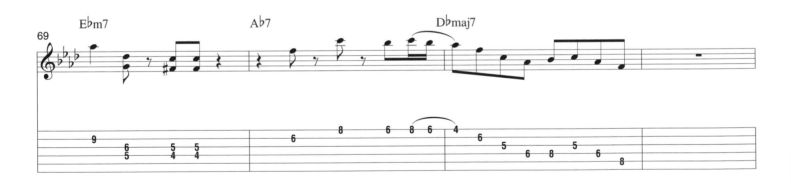

LOVER MAN (OH, WHERE CAN YOU BE?)

By Jimmy Davis, Roger Ramirez and Jimmy Sherman

Quintet: Django Reinhardt, guitar; Stephane Grappelli, violin;
Gianni Safred, piano; Carlo Recori, bass; Aurelio de Carolis, drums.

Figure 6—Intro, Head, and Guitar Solo

"Lover Man (Oh, Where Can You Be?)," a perennial favorite among jazz musicians, is given a unique rendition by Django and the Quintette of the Hot Club of France. The intro starts with unaccompanied violin. In measures 2, 4, and 5 Reinhardt adds some sparse chord stabs in response. Things intensify in measures 7–8 as Reinhardt hits a series of chords in a pounding quarter-note rhythm to set up the entrance of the head.

Reinhardt takes liberties with his phrasing of the head, weaving decorative fills around the melody. Expressive devices like slides, bends, and even vibrato (not often used by jazz guitarists) are employed throughout to add color. He even throws in some harmonics (measure 32 beats 2–3) to cap off a section. In measures 19–20 Reinhardt begins his signature flourish of notes with arpeggio-based runs. Similar wide-range arpeggios are used in measures 25–26 and 35–38. A particularly hip arpeggio superimposition occurs in measure 37 with an F major 7♯5 arpeggio played over G7; this creates a colorful G13♯11 sound. As hard as these runs are, remember that Reinhardt played them using only two left-hand fingers—a true virtuoso!

12 Full Band

13 Slow Demo
Gtr. 1 meas. 19-20, 25-27, 35-40

*Played behind the beat.

Guitar Solo

grad. bend

8va
let ring
Harm.

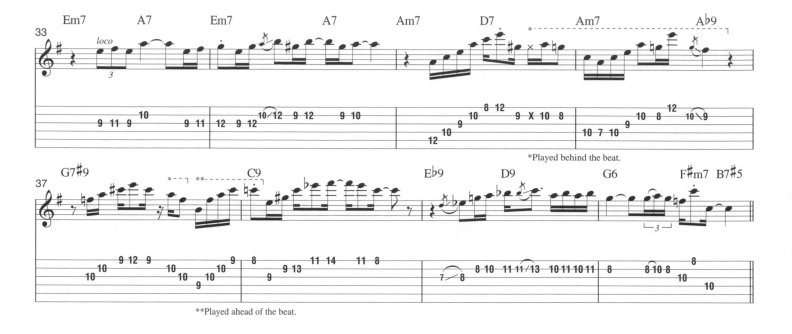

*Played behind the beat.

**Played ahead of the beat.

Figure 7—Violin Solo and Outro

Even with his left-hand ring finger and pinky rendered useless by the tragic fire, Reinhardt would not be stopped. His comping underneath Stephane Grappelli's violin solo is a testament to his tenacity and resourcefulness. He employs his left-hand thumb (notated as "T") as a substitute finger to aid in gripping voicings that require three separate fingers.

For the B section (measures 17–24), a Spanish-sounding pattern consisting of bass note(s) followed by chords in a sixteenth-note triplet rhythm is used to add momentum to the initial B minor sequence. For the next phrase, a chromatic descent in A minor, Reinhardt tremolo-picks the chords for textural contrast and closes the section with a single-note line at the B7 cadence.

The outro is a reprise of the ideas heard in the intro. A lick that alternates fretted notes against an open D-string pedal replaces the intro's quarter-note chords in the penultimate measure.

Fig. 7

1:33

14 Full Band

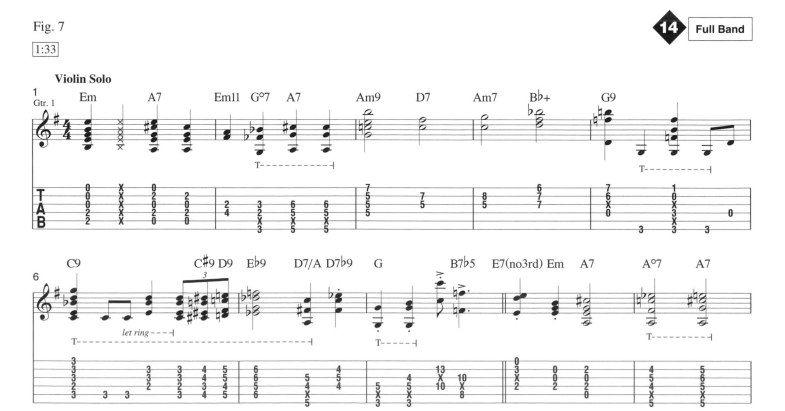

MOONLIGHT IN VERMONT

Words and Music by John Blackburn and Karl Suessdorf

Quintet: Johnny Smith, guitar; Stan Getz, tenor saxophone;
Sanford Gold, piano; Eddie Safranski, bass; Dan Lamond, drums.

Figure 8—Head and Saxophone Solo

Johnny Smith takes an orchestral approach to voicing chords on the guitar. Eschewing the commonly played drop-2 block-chord "grips," Smith voices chords in 3rds and 2nds to approximate a saxophone section. These voicings are lush and colorful but can pose something of a technical nightmare—often times necessitating extreme stretches in the left hand.

For "Moonlight in Vermont," Smith plays a chord-melody arrangement of the head. The tune is transposed to C, a more guitar-friendly key than the original E♭. Smith said, "The hardest thing to do on the guitar is to play a chord melody and play it legato; because there's always that spacing while you're changing chords. Well, by voicing these chords and using the melody on the same string, you can connect these chords and make it sound legato. That's why I did it that way, and I chose a key where I could keep a melody on the same string." Note the chromatic voice leading in measures 6–7 and 26–27, hip 13♭9 chords (derived from the G half-whole diminished scale) sliding up in minor 3rds in measure 20, and the grounding, cadential root-position triads in measures 6, 12, 16, 26, and 32. Stan Getz plays some unobtrusive fills during the head and takes a short solo in measures 27–32.

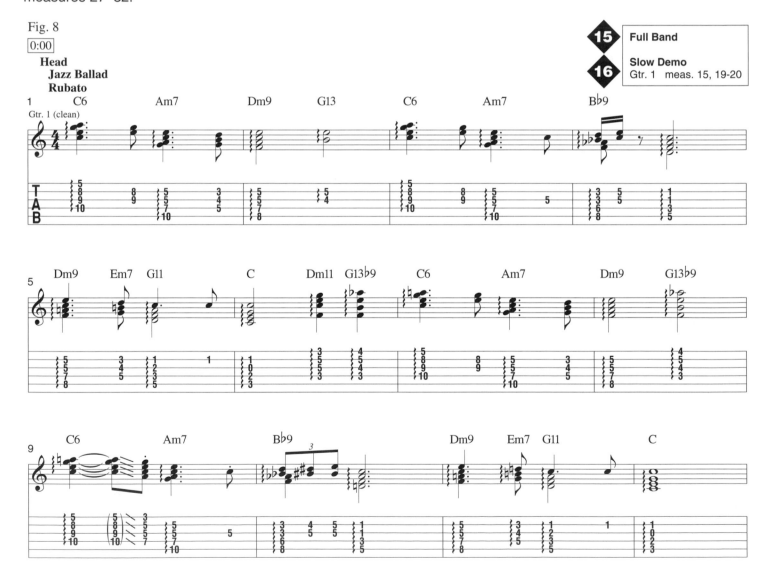

Figure 9—Guitar Solo, Bass Solo, and Coda

Smith's solo on "Moonlight in Vermont" is a classic in the recorded history of jazz guitar and would influence generations of guitarists to come. In his formative years, virtuoso Pat Martino, impressed by the precision and facility of Smith's lines, learned the solo note-for-note (particularly the opening multi-octave Cmaj7 arpeggio run in measure 1). Indeed, Smith's single-note lines were as sophisticated as his chordal work

He creates a gorgeous dissonance in measure 2, beat 4 by superimposing an F# major triad over the G7 chord to yield the #11 (C#), #9 (A#), and major 7 (F#)—an uncommon choice against a dominant chord. In measure 4, over Bb7, he sounds E, the colorful #11 (derived from the Bb Lydian b7 scale: Bb–C–D–E–F–G–Ab) in two octaves to generate mild tension.

During the bass solo (measures 7–14) Smith employs artificial harmonics to create a chiming effect. The sliding 13b9 chords recur in measure 14 and lead back to the theme. The last A section melody is reprised as a coda. In measures 17–18, Stan Getz harmonizes a composed, embellishment figure in 3rds with Smith, which is answered by a descending run in 3rds (not notated here) played by pianist Sandford Gold. The lightning-fast, multi-octave Cmaj7 arpeggio returns in measure 20, foreshadowing the final Cmaj7 chord in measure 22.

Performance Tip: Artificial harmonics are created by lightly touching over the fret wire with the R.H. index finger twelve frets (an octave) higher than a fretted note or open string, and plucking the string with either the right-hand thumb or a pick held by the thumb and middle finger.

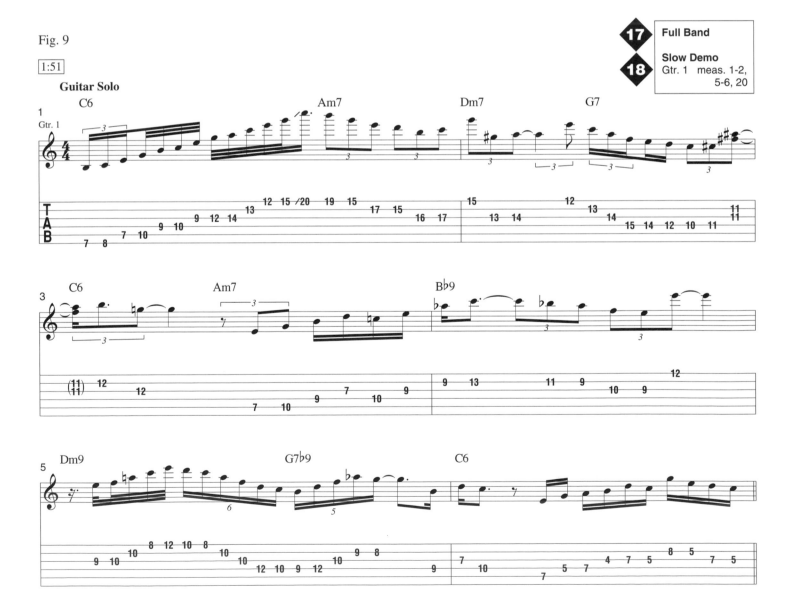

Bass Solo

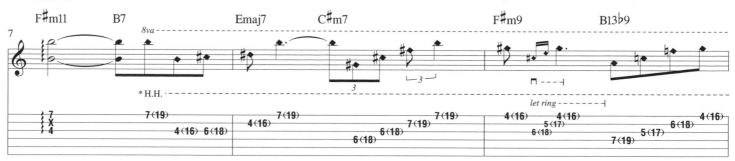

*Fret the note normally, and produce a harmonic by gently resting the pick hand's index finger directly above the indicated fret (in parentheses) while the pick hand's thumb or pick assists by plucking the appropriate string.

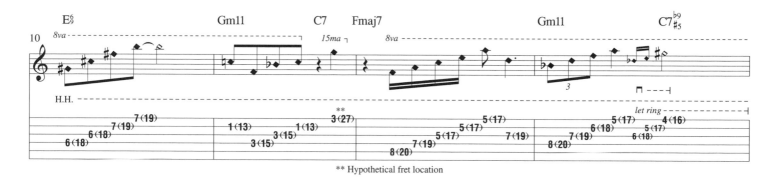

** Hypothetical fret location

Coda

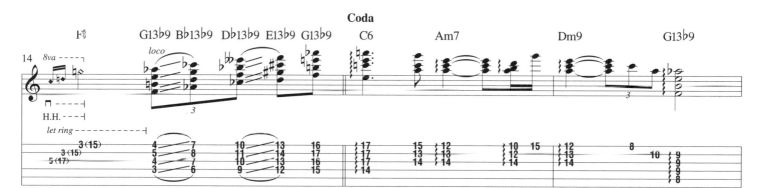

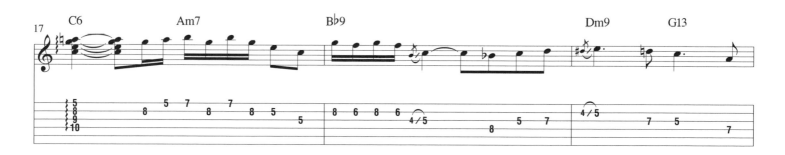

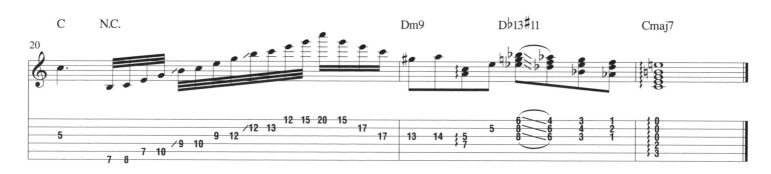

ON A SLOW BOAT TO CHINA

By Frank Loesser

Quintet: Barney Kessel, guitar; Bob Cooper, tenor saxophone;
Claude Williamson, piano; Monty Budwig, bass; Shelly Manne, drums.

Figure 10—Head

In contrast to conventional jazz protocol (the head–solo–solo–head format), Kessel throws in some crafty arranging techniques for the head to "On a Slow Boat to China." He creates interest with the addition of a sequence harmonized in 3rds (harmony part not notated) during measures 15–16 and a composed eight-measure interlude between solos. Kessel wrote the interlude "to provide a send-off for each soloist. It is a little change from the usual procedure of chorus after chorus."

Fig. 10

Figure 11—Interlude and Guitar Solo

Over the eight-measure interlude Kessel starts with eighth-note lines that are motivically unified—the rhythms in measure 2 correspond to the rhythms in measure 4. In measure 7–8, he employs a three-against-four repeating pattern that leads into the solo proper.

Kessel's solo offers a treasure trove of stylistic jazz phrases. A Charlie Parker–inspired chromatic targeting figure played in the head recurs in various configurations in measures 10, 12, 15–16, 20, 31–32, and 36. This figure is one of the most prevalent bop clichés and is an essential lick for the jazz improviser's vocabulary. Other notable moments include the decorated chromatic ascent from B♭ to C across measures 13–15 and the phrase sequencing in measures 25–28.

Fig. 11

1:50

Guitar Solo

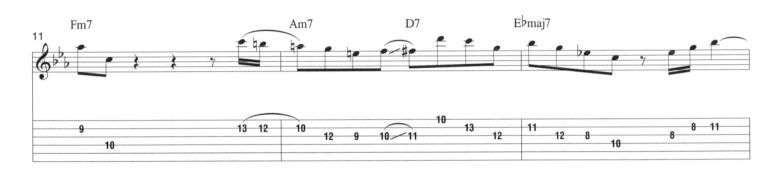

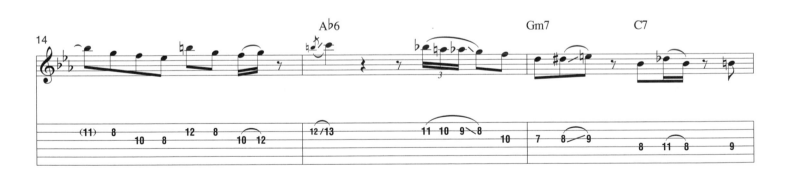

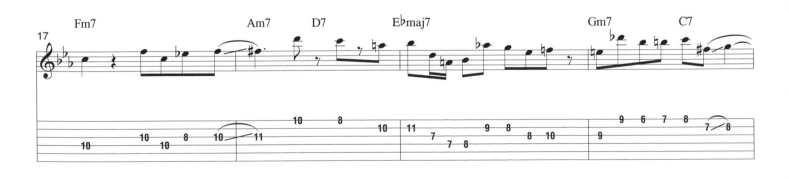

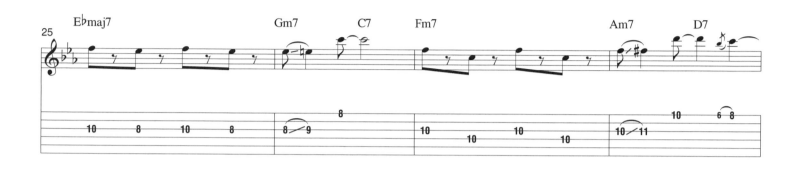

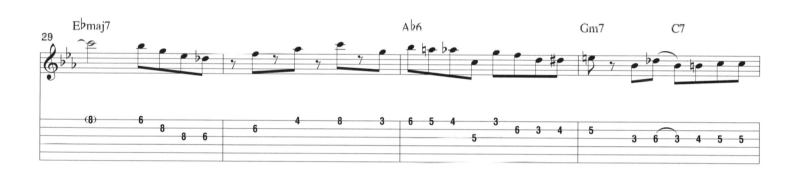

SPEAK LOW

from the Musical Production ONE TOUCH OF VENUS

Words by Ogden Nash
Music by Kurt Weill
Quartet: Grant Green, guitar; Hank Mobley, tenor saxophone;
  Larry Young, organ; Elvin Jones, drums.

Figure 12—Head

After an eight-measure drum intro by Elvin Jones, Green plays the melody of "Speak Low." One of the best aspects of Green's playing is his relaxed feel, evident even here at this brisk tempo. In the A section, Green phrases the melody with staccato accents (the G in measures 2, 4, and 5) and contrasts this with a more legato feel, via hammer-ons, pull-offs, and slides, for the B section.

Figure 13—Guitar Solo

Grant Green is known for his funky, laid-back style, which is more about swinging than burning. In *JazzTimes* magazine, George Benson opined that Green "never got the proper credit because Grant wasn't a speed demon." Green's solo on "Speak Low" proves, however, that when Green wants to, he can really tear it up.

From the get-go he takes an uncompromising, virtuosic approach, starting off in measure 1 with a signature chromatic hammer-on figure that resurfaces throughout the solo (measures 7, 9, 11, 16, 33, 55, 84) and adds a horn-like legato effect. Throughout the course of the solo Green invents simple motives and develops them via compositional devices such as fragmentation (measures 16–20, 77–81), repetition (measures 21–22, 72–77), sequencing (measures 93–94), and rhythmic variation (measures 39–44).

In measures 65–71 Green creates a three-against-four hemiola by repeating a three-note fragment throughout the progression, altering notes as needed to accommodate the chord changes. Another hemiola occurs in measures 96–100. Green ends his solo with a slick line based on chromatically descending major triads over the ii–V–I progression in measures 109–11. Note the "outside" effect of the Ab (functioning as a tritone substitute for D, the dominant of Gm7) and Gb (functioning as a tritone substitute for C, the dominant of F) triads, and the perfect resolution of the F triad.

Fig. 13

2:44

Guitar Solo

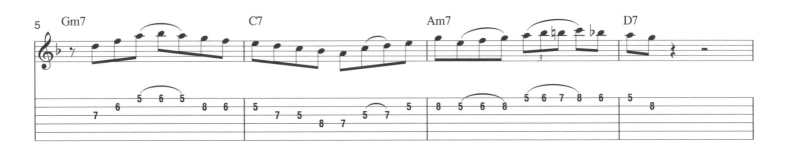

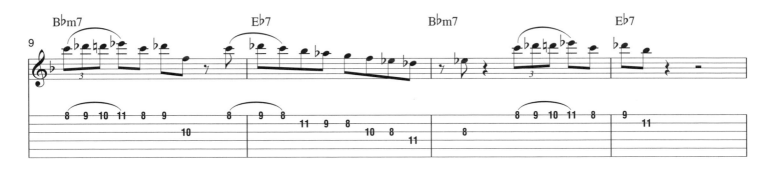

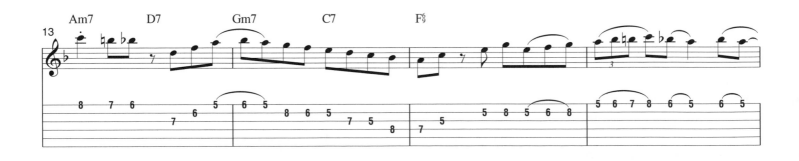

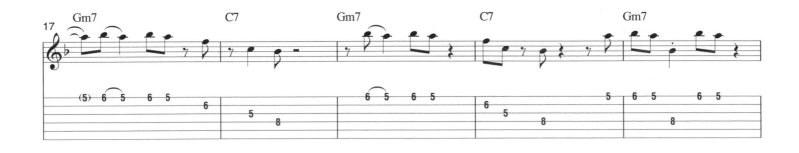

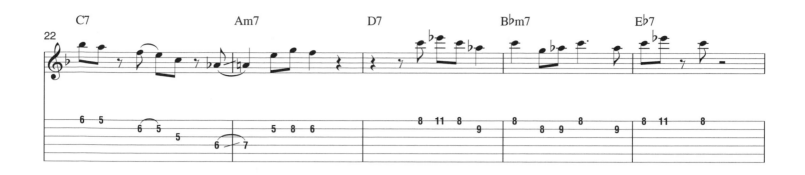

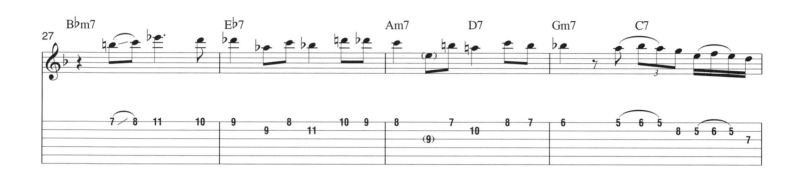

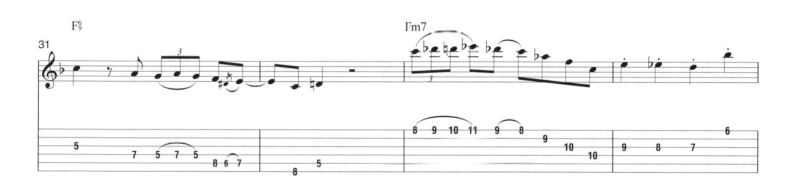

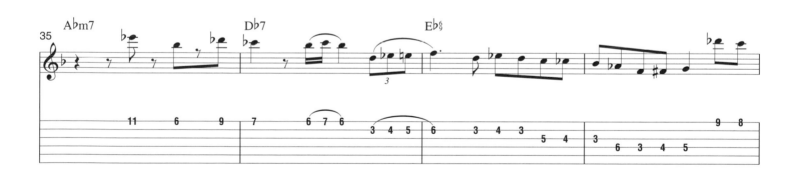

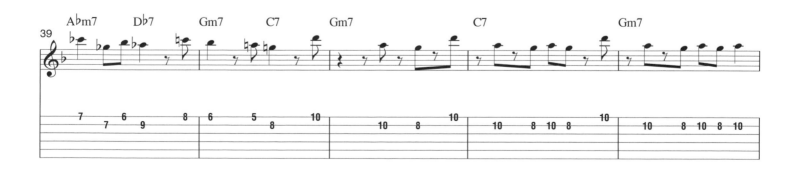

45

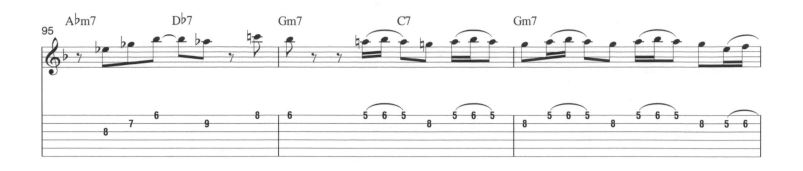

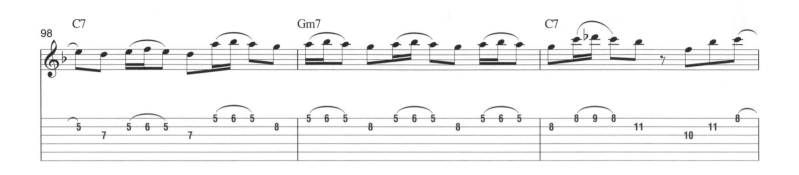

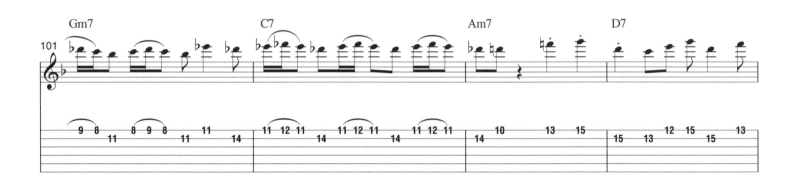

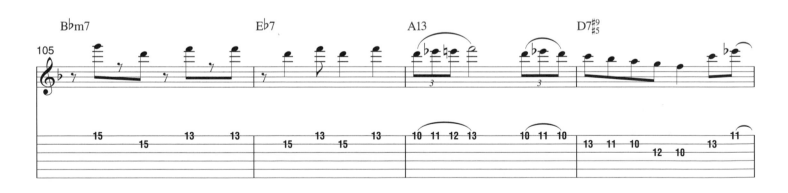

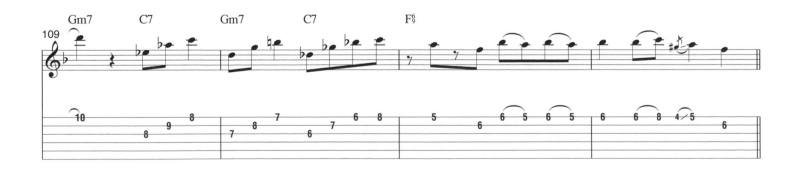

Figure 14—Coda

The coda begins with Green making a definitive statement while using an economy of notes. With the note D as a focal point, Green first simply repeats it with a highly active rhythm (measures 4–6), then adds another note (F) into the mix and alternates between the two (measures 7–11). The F is then displaced down an octave (measure 12) setting up a phrase mixing low- and high-register D notes (measures 14–17).

From measure 18 on, the long lines and the signature, chromatic hammer-on figure resurfaces. As the coda is based solely on the ubiquitous ii–V–III–VI progression, all the great licks here can be put to immediate use once learned.

STOMPIN' AT THE SAVOY

By Benny Goodman, Edgar Sampson and Chick Webb

Trio: Jim Hall, guitar; Carl Perkins, piano; Red Mitchell, bass.

Figure 15—Head and Guitar Solo

Jim Hall's outstanding performance on the standard "Stompin' at the Savoy" is a testament to his creative powers. His rendition of the head (a thirty-two-measure AABA form) incorporates subtle nuances that keep things interesting. Notice how, for the second and last A sections, he manipulates the rhythm by accentuating the upbeats and using staccato phrasing. In measures 15–16 (and measure 59 during the solo) he exploits the slight timbral contrasts of unison notes played on adjacent strings. This technique is similar to a saxophonist's use of alternate fingerings. The B section (measures 17–24) is played chord-melody style, in sharp contrast to the exclusive use of single-notes in the A section.

One signature aspect of Hall's style is his use of legato phrasing. Hall uses devices like hammer-ons, pull-offs, sweep picking, slides, and dynamic contrast to attain a horn-like fluidity. As opposed to some players who pick nearly every note, Hall's articulation is always musical and never sounds stiff or mechanical.

His solo begins over a stop-time figure played by the rhythm section. The band's re-entrance at the B section (measure 49) is punctuated by Hall's use of slides. Hall's compositional soloing approach is evident here. Notice how his solo develops with each idea organically melding into the next. The solo contains a balance of rhythmic ideas (measure 34–44 and 70–79), bluesy phrasing (measures 40–41, 56–66, and 68–70), and intervallic leaps (measures 54–55 and 85–86). The solo concludes with an eight-measure phrase based on double- and triple-stops.

Fig. 15

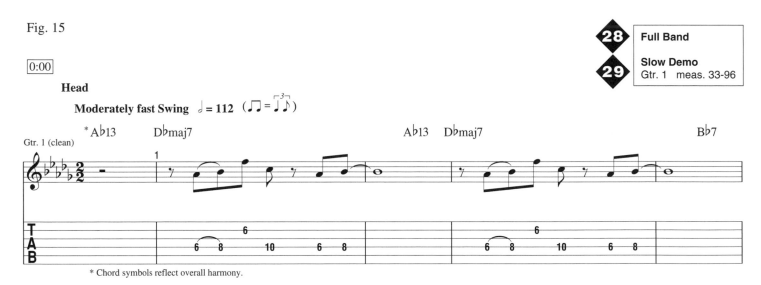

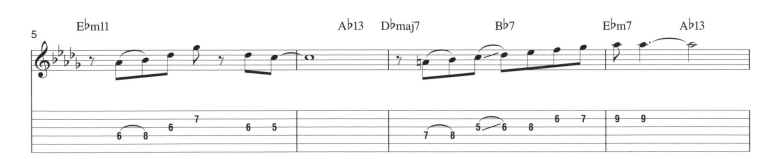

* Chord symbols reflect overall harmony.

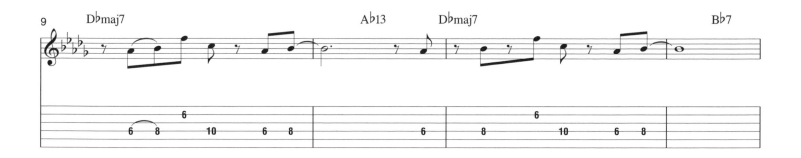

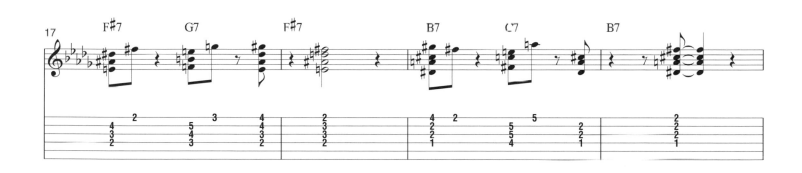

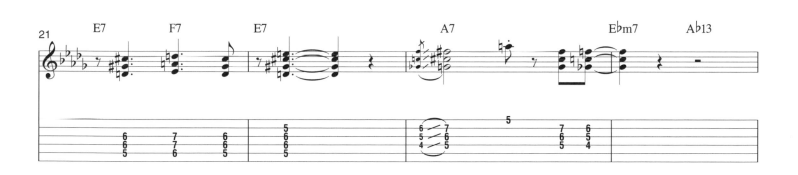

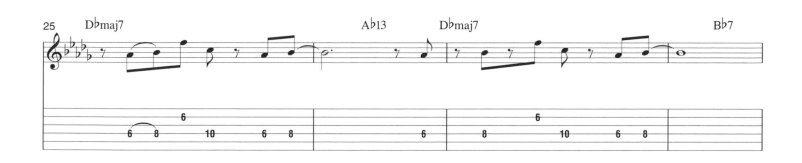

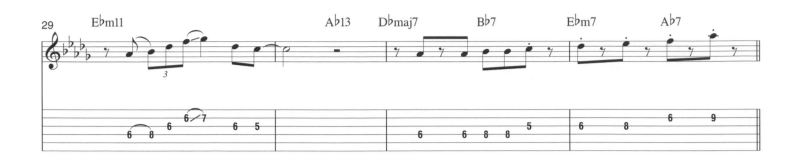

Guitar Solo

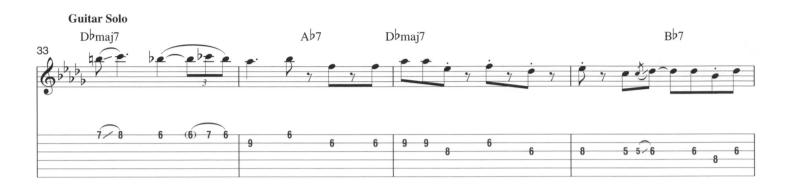

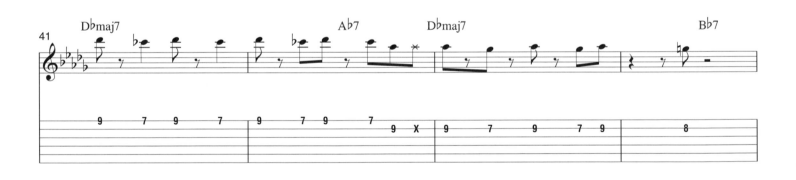

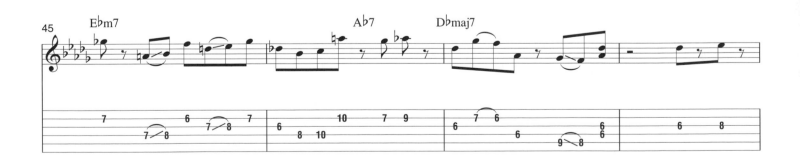

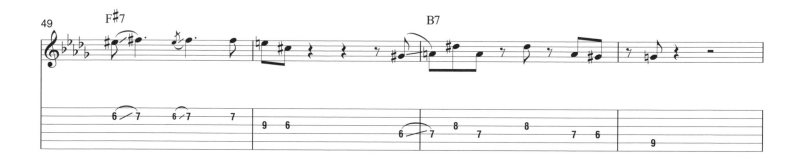

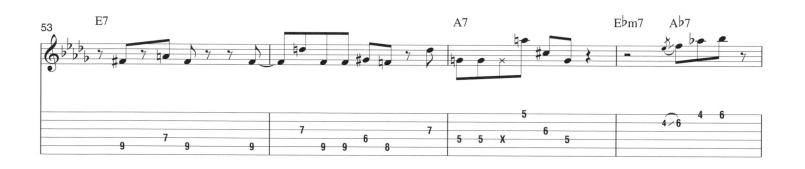

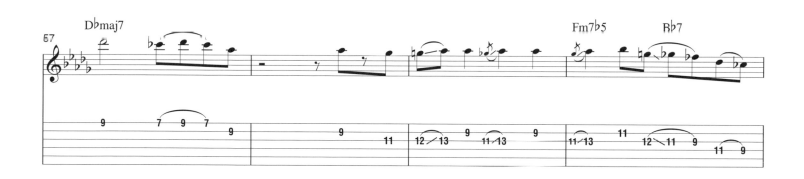

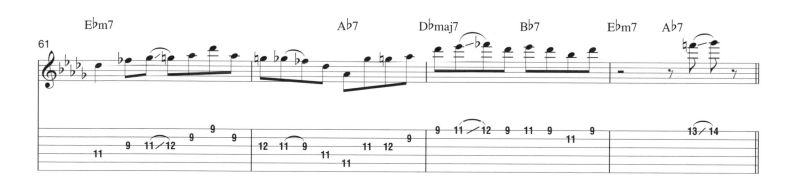

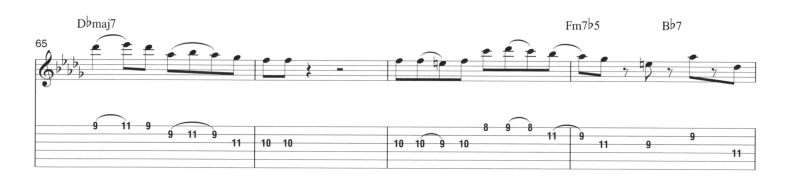

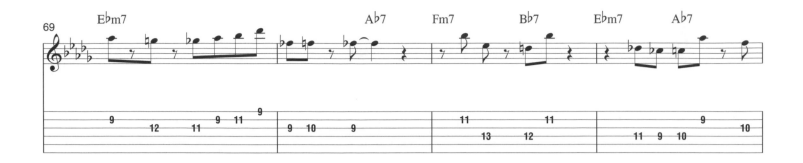

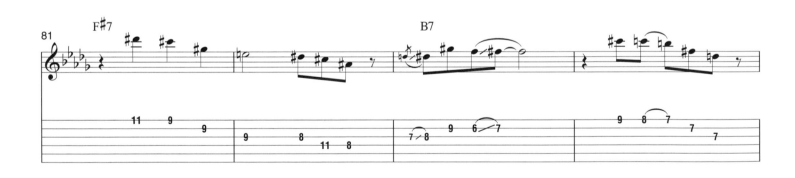

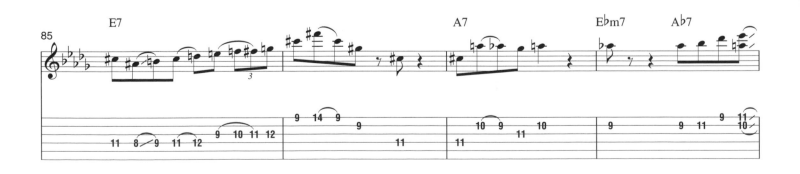

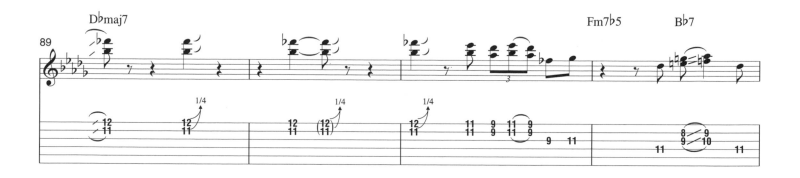

Figure 16—Head Out

Hall adds some neat twists to his rendition of the head out. For the B section, he opts to keep it all single-note melodies, as opposed to the chord phrases played in the opening head. Here, he uses lower half-step approach notes in measures 17–18 and 21 to slide into target notes. This is followed by an ear-catching three-against-four phrase in measures 21–24. A bluesy phrase in measures 30–33 closes out the tune.

Fig. 16

3:23

30 Full Band

31 Slow Demo
Gtr. 1   meas. 1-8,
          17-24, 30-33

THERE IS NO GREATER LOVE

Words by Marty Symes
Music by Isham Jones
Trio: Tal Farlow, guitar; Eddie Costa, piano; Vinnie Burke, bass.

Figure 17—Head and Guitar Solo

"There Is No Greater Love," with its cyclical progression and up-tempo thrust, serves as perfect foil for Tal Farlow's incendiary soloing style. Farlow carves right through the changes and really tears it up on this one. This rendition is played in the key of G, transposed from the more commonly played key of B♭.

Connecting fills like the ones in measures 2–3, 10–11, and 26–27 (all variants) and the ear-catching hemiola in measures 19–21 all serve to embellish the melody. Farlow's decoration of the head should be particularly enlightening to novice jazz musicians who often play jazz heads exactly as written on a lead sheet.

Farlow starts his solo with a three-against-four repeating-type figure that morphs into a D half-whole diminished scale (D–E♭–F–F♯–G♯–A–B–C) run over the break in measures 30–31. More rhythmic manipulation occurs in measures 38–42 and 59–61. This is contrasted with the grounding bluesy phrases in measures 72–76 and 94–97, and the double stops on beats 2 and 4 of measures 83–85. In measures 59–61, Farlow plays a hip, modern-sounding lick based on 13♭9♯9 arpeggio fragments descending in half steps that would be perfectly at home in a John Scofield or Michael Brecker solo.

Full Band

Slow Demo
Gtr. 1   meas. 31-37,
39-47, 49-55,
57-63, 65-70,
77-79, 86-93

Fig. 17

0:00

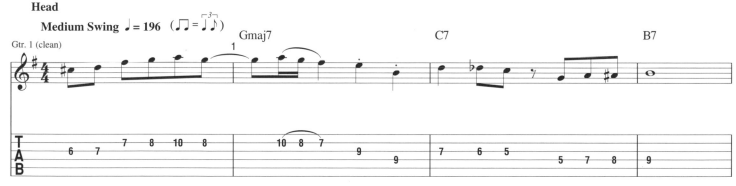

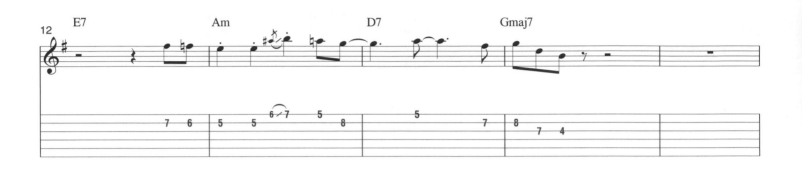

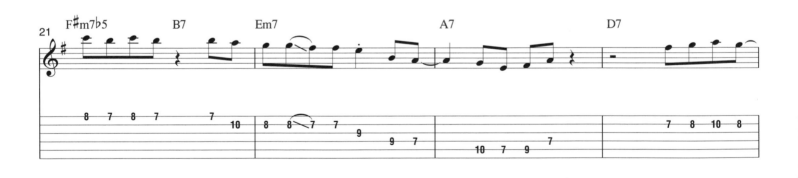

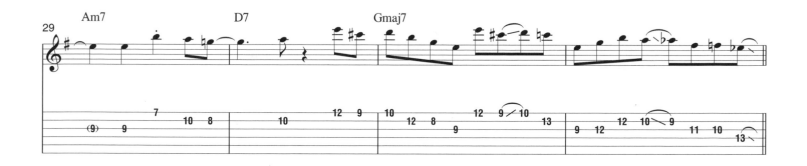

Guitar Solo

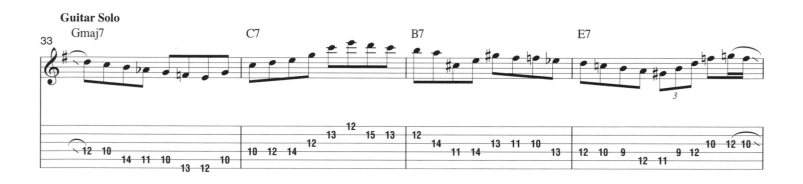

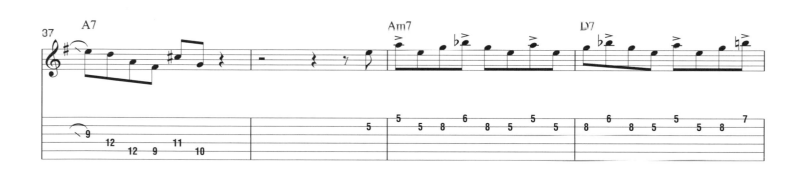

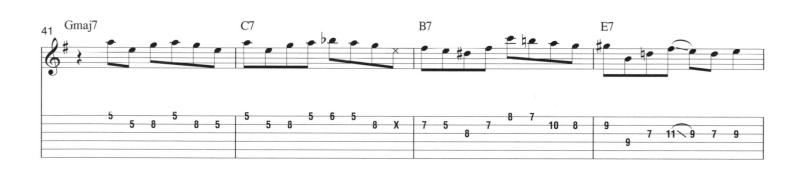

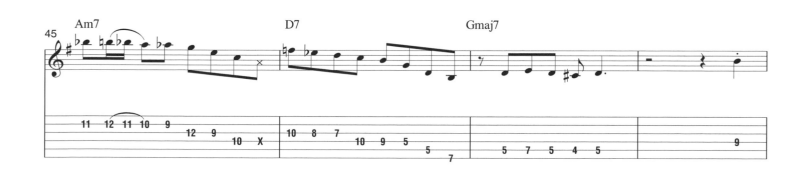

THE WAY YOU LOOK TONIGHT

from SWING TIME

Words by Dorothy Fields
Music by Jerome Kern
Trio: Wes Montgomery, guitar; Mel Rhyne, organ; George Brown, drums.

Figure 18—Head and Guitar Solo

Montgomery preferred using his right-hand thumb to articulate notes. This produced a warm, round sound that has been praised and highly emulated. Interestingly, he came to use his thumb serendipitously; when he started practicing at home with an amplifier, the loud sound produced with the pick disturbed his neighbors. He used his thumb to get a softer sound, and this ended up being his preferred way of playing.

For the head to "The Way You Look Tonight" Montgomery obscures the A section melody by interjecting scalar passages inspired by the original melody. Octaves cap off the last four measures of each A section. For the B section, Montgomery starts by playing the melody (measures 19–23), but for the remainder of the section he lets loose with some great bebop lines. In measure 28, Montgomery plays a stock ii–V lick over the F#m7–B7 change and repeats the lick again in the next measure, this time a half-step lower, to imply an Fm7–B♭7 change (over the B♭m7 chord). This lick is repeated one more time down a half step to imply an Em7–A7 change (over the E♭7 chord) that resolves to A♭maj7 in measure 31. Montgomery finishes off the head playing the A section with the scalar lines as before.

Typically, Montgomery uses a formulaic strategy for soloing. His solos usually start with single-note lines, then octaves, and finally move to a chord solo. This modular approach generates intensity via the increase in harmonic density. In his solo for "The Way You Look Tonight" however, Montgomery abandons his signature soloing blueprint, opting to just tear it up with burning single-note lines.

Montgomery had a highly developed sense of rhythm and would often play rhythmic games with melodies. In measures 116–118, his phrasing implies 3/4 against the underlying 4/4 meter. For measures 119–126, Montgomery divides an eight-measure phrase into two sections; the first four measures consist of a simple, metrically-lucid motive that is repeated verbatim four times. For the next four measures, Montgomery plays a series of arpeggiated chords phrased in a three-against-four rhythm. Another interesting rhythmic phrase occurs in measures 144–145, with rests disguising a three-against-four idea.

Harmonically, Montgomery could take it outside as well. In measure 34, he superimposes an A triad over the C7 chord to create a 13♭9 sound. In measure 69, over Gm7, he momentarily side slips up a half step to A♭ minor and returns on the downbeat of the next measure. Other outside harmonic moves occur in measures 123–124 (E♭ minor triad over D7), 126 (A♭7 arpeggio fragment over C7), and 140 (Fm7 arpeggio over D7). These harmonic detours are balanced throughout the solo by Montgomery's catchy blues melodies.

Fig. 18

34 **Full Band**

35 **Slow Demo**
Gtr. 1   meas. 19-34, 53-56, 64-70,
73-77, 90-102, 105-109, 123-134,
135-137, 146-158, 163-167, 174-182

[0:00]

Head

Fast Swing ♩ = 129 (♫ = ♩♪³)

* Chord symbols reflect basic harmony.

**Play as even quarter notes, 2nd time.

* Played behind the beat.

GUITAR *signature licks*

Signature Licks book/CD packs provide a step-by-step breakdown of "right from the record" riffs, licks, and solos so you can jam along with your favorite bands. They contain performance notes and an overview of each artist's or group's style, with note-for-note transcriptions in notes and tab. The CDs feature full-band demos at both normal and slow speeds.

ACOUSTIC CLASSICS
00695864 ....$19.95

BEST OF ACOUSTIC GUITAR
00695640 ....$19.95

AEROSMITH 1973-1979
00695106 ....$22.95

AEROSMITH 1979-1998
00695219 ....$22.95

BEST OF AGGRO-METAL
00695592 ....$19.95

BEST OF CHET ATKINS
00695752 ....$22.95

THE BEACH BOYS DEFINITIVE COLLECTION
00695683 ....$22.95

BEST OF THE BEATLES FOR ACOUSTIC GUITAR
00695453 ....$22.95

THE BEATLES BASS
00695283 ....$22.95

THE BEATLES FAVORITES
00695096 ....$24.95

THE BEATLES HITS
00695049 ....$24.95

BEST OF GEORGE BENSON
00695418 ....$22.95

BEST OF BLACK SABBATH
00695249 ....$22.95

BEST OF BLINK-182
00695704 ....$22.95

BEST OF BLUES GUITAR
00695846 ....$19.95

BLUES GUITAR CLASSICS
00695177 ....$19.95

BLUES/ROCK GUITAR MASTERS
00695348 ....$19.95

KENNY BURRELL
00695830 ....$22.95

BEST OF CHARLIE CHRISTIAN
00695584 ....$22.95

BEST OF ERIC CLAPTON
00695038 ....$24.95

ERIC CLAPTON – THE BLUESMAN
00695040 ....$22.95

ERIC CLAPTON – FROM THE ALBUM UNPLUGGED
00695250 ....$24.95

BEST OF CREAM
00695251 ....$22.95

CREEDANCE CLEARWATER REVIVAL
00695924 ....$22.95

DEEP PURPLE – GREATEST HITS
00695625 ....$22.95

THE BEST OF DEF LEPPARD
00696516 ....$22.95

THE DOORS
00695373 ....$22.95

FAMOUS ROCK GUITAR SOLOS
00695590 ....$19.95

BEST OF FOO FIGHTERS
00695481 ....$22.95

ROBBEN FORD
00695903 ....$22.95

GREATEST GUITAR SOLOS OF ALL TIME
00695301 ....$19.95

BEST OF GRANT GREEN
00695747 ....$22.95

GUITAR INSTRUMENTAL HITS
00695309 ....$19.95

GUITAR RIFFS OF THE '60S
00695218 ....$19.95

BEST OF GUNS N' ROSES
00695183 ....$22.95

HARD ROCK SOLOS
00695591 ....$19.95

JIMI HENDRIX
00696560 ....$24.95

HOT COUNTRY GUITAR
00695580 ....$19.95

BEST OF JAZZ GUITAR
00695586 ....$24.95

ERIC JOHNSON
00699317 ....$24.95

ROBERT JOHNSON
00695264 ....$22.95

THE ESSENTIAL ALBERT KING
00695713 ....$22.95

B.B. KING – THE DEFINITIVE COLLECTION
00695635 ....$22.95

THE KINKS
00695553 ....$22.95

BEST OF KISS
00699413 ....$22.95

MARK KNOPFLER
00695178 ....$22.95

LYNYRD SKYNYRD
00695872 ....$24.95

BEST OF YNGWIE MALMSTEEN
00695669 ....$22.95

BEST OF PAT MARTINO
00695632 ....$22.95

WES MONTGOMERY
00695387 ....$24.95

BEST OF NIRVANA
00695483 ....$24.95

THE OFFSPRING
00695852 ....$24.95

VERY BEST OF OZZY OSBOURNE
00695431 ....$22.95

BEST OF JOE PASS
00695730 ....$22.95

PINK FLOYD – EARLY CLASSICS
00695566 ....$22.95

THE POLICE
00695724 ....$22.95

THE GUITARS OF ELVIS
00696507 ....$22.95

BEST OF QUEEN
00695097 ....$24.95

BEST OF RAGE AGAINST THE MACHINE
00695480 ....$24.95

RED HOT CHILI PEPPERS
00695173 ....$22.95

RED HOT CHILI PEPPERS – GREATEST HITS
00695828 ....$24.95

BEST OF DJANGO REINHARDT
00695660 ....$24.95

BEST OF ROCK
00695884 ....$19.95

BEST OF ROCK 'N' ROLL GUITAR
00695559 ....$19.95

BEST OF ROCKABILLY GUITAR
00695785 ....$19.95

THE ROLLING STONES
00695079 ....$24.95

BEST OF JOE SATRIANI
00695216 ....$22.95

BEST OF SILVERCHAIR
00695488 ....$22.95

THE BEST OF SOUL GUITAR
00695703 ....$19.95

BEST OF SOUTHERN ROCK
00695560 ....$19.95

ROD STEWART
00695663 ....$22.95

BEST OF SURF GUITAR
00695822 ....$19.95

BEST OF SYSTEM OF A DOWN
00695788 ....$22.95

STEVE VAI
00673247 ....$22.95

STEVE VAI – ALIEN LOVE SECRETS: THE NAKED VAMPS
00695223 ....$22.95

STEVE VAI – FIRE GARDEN: THE NAKED VAMPS
00695166 ....$22.95

STEVE VAI – THE ULTRA ZONE: NAKED VAMPS
00695684 ....$22.95

STEVIE RAY VAUGHAN
00699316 ....$24.95

THE GUITAR STYLE OF STEVIE RAY VAUGHAN
00695155 ....$24.95

BEST OF THE VENTURES
00695772 ....$19.95

THE WHO
00669561 ....$22.95

BEST OF ZZ TOP
00695738 ....$24.95

Complete descriptions and songlists online!

FOR MORE INFORMATION, SEE YOUR LOCAL MUSIC DEALER, OR WRITE TO:

HAL•LEONARD® CORPORATION
7777 W. BLUEMOUND RD. P.O. BOX 13819 MILWAUKEE, WI 53213

www.halleonard.com

Prices, contents and availability subject to change without notice.

0308